A TIME TO CONSIDER

TIM SWEETMAN

Scripture references are from the following bible translations:

TPT

ERV

Foreword - by Hazel Sweetman

I thoroughly enjoyed reading this book.

It's an easy book to read but very challenging for each of us.

Where is our life headed?

Do we know?

If not then this is the book for you.....

If we believe that we know then perhaps there is more for us to think about?

A time for us to consider.

Acknowledgements

In putting together this book I would like to give a big thank you to my brother John who is always ready to assist with punctuation, correction and script editing.

Also to Haze! who is able to find grammar and spelling corrections no matter how many times I search beforehand.

My greatest thanks goes to Father who always inspires and leads me into placing words on paper.

Without His permanent presence, whispering how the next line should go there would be no book.

Thank you.

A Time To Consider

Occasionally there appears a brief moment in our lives when we have time to pause and consider where we are heading and why.

This short book aims to answer some of those questions.

....

Preface:

'A Time To Consider' was written at a time when several friends and friends of friends had been taken Ill by potentially life threatening illnesses.

When this happens to us out of the blue it is naturally a shocking discovery to realize that we aren't going to live on this earth, in this body, for ever.

It is however a reality that we all need to take into consideration.

Any of us may be taken away at any time.

Our life on earth is a very short period when we consider eternity.

Let us get involved with eternity now - we may not get another opportunity to do so.

A note from the Author

Hi,

Thanks for reading this book. You will enjoy it.

I have written other books.

'A Journey into Life' was written for those curious about how to gain entry to Gods Kingdom and what to expect when they arrive.

'Some Adjustments Required?' was written for those who believed that they had arrived in Gods Kingdom and perhaps had not and also for those who like many of us had settled for less than we should rightfully have.

This Book – **'A Time To Consider'** is written specifically for you.

Chapters

Life

What use is it if we gain the whole world but lose our own soul?

Mk. 8.36

Many of us live our busy lives through to the end without giving a serious thought as to what might happen to us after our bodies die.

If we do stop at times to wonder about these things then our thoughts end with unanswered questions or theories that lead nowhere.

For many, it is not until we are pulled up in our tracks perhaps by the onset of a life changing illness or a trauma of some sort that we really begin to wonder what this life is all about.

I believe that it is the hand of God who allows the situations that cause us to stop and think.

God cares far more about our eternity and our character than our comfort and temporary health issues.

In terms of eternity, it is the ones who stop in life to consider their frailty and temporality in life on this earth that are in many ways the better off as they have the opportunity to ask those important questions and to receive answers if they know where to ask.

Some people appear to sail through life without a care or worry. It is these people who fail to stop to consider the really crucial factors of life itself.

For so many, life may end suddenly and unexpectedly without having taken the opportunity to stop and take stock.

These busy people travel through life and then are gone.

You my friend have this moment in time, and it may only be a brief moment, in order to change your life for all time.

For you a window of opportunity has opened up. God has set this time aside for you to discover Him.

Consider that for just one minute if you would.

God cares about you so much that He has arranged for you to find out about Him.

This may not be the first time that He has introduced Himself to you but this may be the last and is a one time opportunity for you that God has chosen and it is an opportunity that is unique to you.

How will you respond to His invitation?

Will you take this time to discover the reality of God?

I have written this book so that you can have some of those difficult questions answered.

It is sometimes hard for us to approach what might be a complete stranger and begin a conversation with questions such as, "what is life all about"?

Or even

"What will happen to me after death"?

For many of us that is where we are in our lives. We would like to begin that conversation but where to start? And who to ask?

Some of us are natural 'mixers', we know how to strike up a conversation and can easily break the ice with those very conversation starters - although not easily I guess?

But then, once the conversation begins, we have to ask, does the person I am talking to have any better idea than I do?

Do we begin with a bright and breezy, "Hi, how are you? Or should we start with a more formal greeting?

Our culture often dictates the manner in which we might greet another person.

In the west the tendency is to make a formal handshake and then to quickly step away.

Elsewhere a kiss on the cheek is the norm.

In another part of the world perhaps an embrace would be normal and in some cultures the rubbing of noses is appropriate.

This doesn't happen in the UK often but I sometimes watch on news items people in other countries sitting around in the sun chatting perhaps in cafes and wonder whether they are discussing life or just passing the time.

Whilst we might eventually, but rarely do, talk about these things theoretically with each other, we may never come to any sound conclusions and who knows where those answers are anyway?

So who knows?

Who can we ask?

Where will we find the truth?

There is only one true authority on life and He is the one who created life from the beginning, long before man's existence.

The one who initiated that *'big bang'* as the scientists like to currently refer to it.

God is the ultimate answer and also holds the keys to all of the subsequent and related questions and answers as well.

He has given us a lot of answers, some of them are to be found in a book called the Bible.

I will be referring to it as we go.

Can we rely on God?

Does He Exist? - Then Prove It!

I have been asked on many occasions to prove the existence of the God that I believe and trust in.

Let me begin to give those who question His reality an answer.

God is Spirit – He is invisible.

However, we know that God exists by His interaction with man down through the ages.

God leaves His handprint upon our history.

We can also see God's character of love in the life of His son Jesus.

There are several Christian apologists who can argue for the existence of God all day long citing nature, biology, science etc.

There are others who point to the nation of Israel - itemising their impossible struggle for becoming a nation and the fact that they exist.

I know of many people who are able to point to their own experience of God. Perhaps they have been miraculously healed from an incurable disease. Perhaps they have been miraculously released from addictions or drug use.

God has brought miraculous changes in the lives of gangland leaders and drug barons and millions of ordinary people like you and I.

Whole nations have been delivered from oppression as a result of appealing to God.

In our own nation of Britain we can look back and see how thousands of soldiers were transported from Dunkirk during ww2 after the whole country were called to prayer – an impossible task but accomplished with little loss of life. During that event alone we can see God's hand in providing cloud cover, convenient weather conditions, a willingness for boatmen of all description from around the coast to provide transport.

God uses many and various ways in order to answer when we call on Him.

Others have found release from slavery and terrible, unthinkable, abuses after placing their trust in God.

All of these events and incidents are tangible proof of God.

We can also look at Jesus whose earthly life can be verified by thousands of eye witnesses. Independent historians with no affiliation to the Christian faith, alive at that time, wrote about Him.

After His death and resurrection hundreds of people met with Him and also wrote about their experiences and we can find no voice of dissent from their eye witness reports.

Those who followed Jesus suffered intolerable pain, torture and death simply because they chose to speak about Him.

Do we believe that each one of them would have chosen to suffer in that way if what they had said about His resurrection was a lie?

Surely one of them would have given the game away at the last had what they said not been true?

To suffer Roman torture for the truth is one thing but how many would give their lives and their family's lives up for a lie?

The changed lives alone speak volumes about the existence of God and His hand in our lives.

Some have been transported to heaven and returned to speak of Him.

Others have seen and spoken to angels.

Many millions of us know Him personally and can verify His hand and His love in our lives.

The list is endless when we take the time and trouble to look into the ways of God and His dealings with mankind.

Yet, despite all of these infallible proofs and witness reports – enough evidence to convict a murderer in a court of law - I still hear the taunt, 'if you can prove He exists, I will believe in Him'.

The truth behind this statement is that we desperately need to absolve ourselves from any responsibility.

By challenging God to prove Himself we are mentally clearing ourselves from our responsibility to find Him.

'if you're there God, then show yourself to me'.

The absence of any visible reality in response to our challenge then relieves us in our deceived mind of our situation.

We reason that when at the end of life God asks us to account for ourselves we can glibly reply, 'well I asked you to show yourself and you didn't'.

God doesn't normally respond to us in that way - He is not someone who is at our beck and call.

We need to understand that from the beginning of our relationship with Him – He is God.

God longs for us to know Him personally and intimately but I suspect that if He went around showing Himself to us we would probably die of shock – overwhelmed by His glory.

God showed His glory partly to Moses on the mountain when He was talking to Moses about the commandments but He only revealed His back parts and even then Moses was severely changed.

Then the Lord said to Moses, "I will do what you ask. I will do this because I am pleased with you and because I know you very well."

Then Moses said, "Now, please show me your Glory." Then the Lord answered, "I will show my love and mercy to anyone I want to.

So I will cause my perfect goodness to pass by in front of you, and I will speak my name, YAHWEH, so that you can hear it. But you cannot see my face.

No one can see me and continue to live."

Then the Lord said, "Here is a place for you to stand by me on this large rock. I will put you in a large crack in that rock. Then I will cover you with my hand, and my Glory will pass by. Then I will take away my hand, and you will see my back. But you will not see my face."

Exodus 33:17-23 ERV

God does however reveal Himself through His actions and in the life of His son Jesus.

His actions and interactions with man's existence on earth have been detailed in many ways through the ages.

His personal relationships with individuals on earth are well known and many pages of writing have been put on paper telling us of these relationships and yet we still challenge God to prove Himself as if He is a man with something to prove.

Many hours have been expended in detailing the life of Jesus.

Jesus showed God's character while He was on earth – God is Love.

No one has ever characterised God's love in the way that Jesus was able to.

God showed Himself to mankind through Jesus.

God who is immortal – omnipresent – invincible – unfathomable – magnificent, chose to reveal Himself to us through Jesus.

Now then given who God is – why would He do that?

He has nothing to prove to us.

God does not need to defend Himself.

But He is Love.

His patience far outweighs our cynicism and our doubt and our insecurity and our fear and our arrogance.

If we want to know if God is, then we need to come to Him in humility realising the immensity of who He is and ask Him to help our lack of belief.

He understands our inadequacies.

When we come to Him in honesty, searching for truth, then He is pleased to make Himself known to us.

It is His desire for us to not only know Him but to come right into the middle of His amazing presence.

The key is honesty - a searching heart.

God rewards a humble person.

God will always oppose our arrogance.

Who are we to challenge God?

Our challenge of 'prove yourself to me' will not carry much weight when we are called to account for ourselves.

What have we done with our lives?

Have we taken time to know God?

The responsibility is ours – God has done all He can in order to bridge that gap – He sent His only Son in love to die for us.

God will sometimes step into our life with an invitation for us to discover Him.

This is such an invitation.

How will we respond to that?

The Bible – Can we believe what it says?

The Bible has been called 'God's book'.

I like to refer to it as God's letter of love to us.

It is a book that has many authors who all write upon the same subject throughout – God's eternal love for us - His creation.

The Bible is an account of God's dealings with man and span a period from the beginning of all things until on into eternity.

The Bible is a book that has been written and put together under the inspiration of The Spirit of God who is Holy and can not lie.

Within the Bible is the moral basis for the whole of mankind – our societies are built upon its structure.

If we cannot rely on the truth of the Bible then we cannot rely on anything in the whole of the cosmos and we are in deep despair.

There have been many translations of the Bible from the original text into various languages. Some of these translations are better than others.

Some interpretations better match the original thinking than others.

The Bible has been interpreted by people who make mistakes and misjudgements as we all do from time to time. It is therefore our own responsibility in line with what God is saying to us personally to ascertain the truth within the text according to the original author's intention.

The Bible tells us about the heartbeat of God – His enduring desire for true relationship with us His children.

The Bible is a book that we can depend upon totally.

Religion

Let us now return to the reason that we are here.

We are looking for answers aren't we?

What is life all for?

It is not often that we stop and think about these things at all but when we do the cause is sometimes as a result of the death of a loved one or some critical illness that has stopped us in our tracks.

We have been given a brief moment in time to consider our situation.

When we are looking for answers about the meaning and purpose of life – where are we now and also what happens afterwards, the first port of call is sometimes a religious organisation of one type or another.

My purpose here is not to get you involved in a religious organisation.

There may well be some Christians that are able to point you in the right direction but my fear is that you may also be seduced by the organisation that they belong to.

Therefore I won't introduce you to church but I will introduce you to Jesus.

Jesus came in order to bring us freedom from religiosity – He came in order to give us life and freedom from that and any other type of bondage.

We can read about the relevance of church or the lack of it later.

Jesus came to bring us answers, which is handy because answers are what we are looking for too, aren't they?

So who is this Jesus? We've heard rumours about Him but what did He really do?

Jesus changed everything.

First Things First

We are jumping ahead of ourselves a bit here. In order for me to tell you about who Jesus is and what He did I need to first tell you about why He came.

When we look around us at the way people behave we can see that we are in need of help.

There are some nice people and there are some good people but when we look closer and really get to know them we find that even the good and nice people aren't as wonderful as they seem to be on the surface. Then there are downright bad people.

We know from just looking at our own attitudes of selfishness and bad desires, greed and self pity that we need some help. Don't we?

This hasn't always been the situation though.

The first people on the earth had a great relationship with God.

We can read about it in the book of Genesis ch. 1 and 2 in the bible. But then man rebelled against God and sin began to spoil all of creation.

It has also caused a barrier to come between God and us.

This is why we behave the way that we do – it is because we don't know another way. Sin – all the bad things that we think and do - has become our default way of living.

That original rebellion has affected the way that we live ever since – it is because there is now a division between us and God.

All the time that we are separated from God our thoughts and words and actions become more fragmented and devious because we are apart from the truth that is God.

You can well understand that after such a long time being separated from God our ways have become pretty devious - so bad in fact that we often don't even realise ourselves why we do certain things. Do you recognize that problem?

You might also imagine how God longs again for our company. After all we were brought into the world for the purpose of having a close relationship with God and now we have lost that – He has lost that too.

If you are a parent and have ever experienced a long break away from your children then you know exactly how God feels having been separated from us for so long with no hope of there ever being reconciliation.

These days we rarely give a thought as to what God thinks about or what we do or say.

How His heart must break.

But God had a plan – God always has a plan.

This is why He sent Jesus – His own son who He loved so much into the world in order to redeem us – to buy us back.

There was no way that we could ever get back to God on our own merit. It is impossible for a sinless God to have any relationship with man – sin always gets in the way - but God doesn't want any of us to be lost.

So how could God get rid of that sin? What was there that He could do?

If only there was someone who was without any sin who would be willing to sacrifice himself as a perfect sinless offering then that sacrifice would pay for the redemption of the whole earth.

But was that possible?

A pure and holy and sinless sacrifice? Where was that going to come from?

God loved the world so much that he gave his only Son, so that everyone who believes in him would not be lost but have eternal life.

John 3:16 ERV

Jesus was and is God's only perfect and sinless Son.

Jesus came to the world and lived among us for a while in order to be that perfect sacrifice.

The story of His life, death and resurrection and the reason that He came and all that He was and achieved can be read about in the first four books of the New Testament.

He voluntarily came to earth and suffered rejection and pain and gave Himself up to death solely in order for us to be redeemed to God.

Jesus paid that price for our sakes.

For us the price of our redemption – our being bought back from sin - has been paid by Jesus.

We will always be eternally grateful for that selfless gift, won't we?

Just stop for a minute here and let Him know how grateful we are.

But you know there is more to tell.

Jesus didn't only die in order to pay for us to be reunited with God.

After three days in the depths of the earth Jesus rose again from the dead!

Jesus proved that He had beaten death itself!

Death had taken every person on earth since sin had come into the world as a result of man's rebellion but because Jesus was sinless and perfect - there was no rebellion found in Him - death could not hold Him in its grip. It had no power over Jesus.

Jesus had finally won over death and sin. He had taken the victory and things would never ever be the same again.

How Does That Affect Me?

Forgiveness

Let's read that verse from the Bible that we read earlier again shall we?

God loved the world so much that he gave his only Son, so that everyone who believes in him would not be lost but have eternal life.

John 3:16 ERV

This sounds like an amazing promise doesn't it?

But there is even more hidden within those words.

Allow me to unpack some of it for you.

The word *'Everyone'* is a reference to you and me which appears to be obvious but you would be surprised how many people think that it refers to everyone else.

This is a promise to us personally.

When God sent His only son Jesus to earth to suffer and die He had you in His mind.

Jesus went through all of that for you because God loves you so much that He can't bear to be without you in His presence.

Isn't that amazing?

It makes my hair stand on end just to think about it.

How much Jesus must love us?

He loves us enough to die for us so that we will not be lost. Wow!

When we read the phrase in that verse we tend to think that it means that when we die we can go to heaven but there is so much more than that in there.

What that phrase is actually saying is that we won't be lost but we will receive real life in union with God Himself now.

It means that from this moment we will become one with God in the same way that Jesus is one with God.

Life in union with God isn't the same as the life that we had before.

God isn't saying that we will continue having the same life as before. He is saying that the new life will be an abundant God filled, supernatural life unlike anything that we can imagine and it begins now!

What have we done to deserve such things?

Absolutely nothing.

Jesus has paid the price for us because God chose to give us that life – because He loves us.

There is no other reason.

We can never earn it – it is God's good pleasure to give it to us freely. Wow! Imagine that.

God loves us so much that He wants to make an eternal and unbreakable contract with us.

So what are the conditions for receiving this abundant life now?

We must realise that we are useless sinners and that we are in need of help.

I think we know that, don't we?

We also need to realise that our situation is as a result of our own bad thoughts and behaviour – we need to apologise for that.

When we have realised our sorry state and have a desire for change then God gives us the ability to believe that Jesus' sacrifice is sufficient to pay for our mistakes – our sin. We are able to believe that all that bad stuff that we have done in the past has been removed from our tab and that because of what Jesus has done God sees us as a new creation – holy and sinless just as Jesus is.

Jesus has achieved all of that on our behalf.

The only thing that we need to do is to realise it and to trust that He has done that for us personally.

We are forgiven and God invites us right back into His presence.

God knows about all of our past – yes every part of it.

When we place our lives in His hands trusting that Jesus's sacrifice is sufficient to bring us back to God then all of our past sin is immediately forgiven – all of it - without any exceptions.

It is a wonderful feeling to know that every single bit of our past life has been forgiven completely and utterly.

It's all gone forever. Never to be remembered again.

'Thank you Jesus for doing that for me. I am now redeemed and I can come back to you'.

With God it is always personal.

So why do I need Jesus?

I need Jesus in my life because without Him I tend to make a mess of everything that I do.

Paul wrote:

Here is a true statement that should be accepted without question: Christ Jesus came into the world to save sinners, and I am the worst of them.

1 Timothy 1:15 ERV

That is such a short sentence and easy to read. It sums up in a nutshell the reason that Jesus came to earth.

None of us are perfect. In fact most of us fall a long, long way short of being perfect, you know what I am talking about I think?

But when we place our trust in Jesus a miracle takes place.

God loves us so much that He wants us to be, not just in contact with Him, but to actually become 'one' with Him.

Isn't that incredible? It's very difficult to imagine.

Within that single act of placing our trust in the saving power of Jesus's sacrifice we miraculously become 'one' with God.

You see before we couldn't come close to God, apart from saying a prayer or two from a distance, because we had sin in our lives but once that sin has been removed everything changes!

The whole situation has now altered and we have become a totally new and different creation – we have become sinless because God sees us through the sacrifice of Jesus which took away all of that sin.

The obstacle that was in the way and the cause of our separation from God has been removed!

We become a freed person! We are unique.

Now that we are one with God our minds are freed – we are able to think the thoughts of God.

As our minds are renewed and released from the constraints of sin then our words also reflect those positive and truthful thoughts which are translated into the things that we do – the way we behave – the way we respond to things in our life.

Everything changes – new life has come.

Sin doesn't have any power over us any more – we are freed to behave differently.

Bad relationships can be restored.

Destructive habits can be removed.

Self harming life styles can be altered.

Fears can be replaced with trust and security.

Everything is new – we are a new creation.

Relationships

We talked earlier about church.

A lot of Christians believe that when we ask God to accept us into His Kingdom then we need to start going to church.

The Bible doesn't tell us this.

I have discussed this in my book, 'Some Adjustments Required' more fully but I will briefly explain to you why this is not so.

What the Bible does say is not to stop meeting up with other Christians.

We must not quit meeting together, as some are doing. No, we need to keep on encouraging each other. This becomes more and more important as you see the Day getting closer.

Hebrews 10:25 ERV

This verse has nothing at all to do with attending church.

What the writer to the Hebrew Christians was referring to was the need to keep encouraging each other whenever we meet up. This could be socially or at work or when we are out for a meal or just chatting at home.

Our English word and concept of church doesn't appear anywhere in the original text of the Bible at all – it is no where to be found.

Wherever the English version of the Bible mentions the word 'church' it is a mistranslation and what Jesus and

His followers were really talking about is a group of elected people or a group of people who have been called out for a purpose as a jury or public committee might be.

The translators of the original text into English didn't understand the same relational group of people that Jesus was referring to and so they simply translated the word as 'church' because as they looked around them that was all they knew about.

Jesus and His followers used the Greek word *'Ecclesia'* which as we have said means, 'called out people'.

The translators however didn't understand this concept and so they used instead the word that they did understand which was church, - *'Kuriakos'*.

'Kuriakos' was then used incorrectly throughout the new testament.

The concept of church was not recognised by Jesus or His followers, it was an idea of man's that came much later.

However we are 'called out' of the world to be in relationship with each other.

We need to meet up with others who know Jesus in order to grow and mature and not to be people who sit in a church pew to be preached at.

This relationship might be with the person who gave you this book and others that you know or it might be with individuals from a variety of places. God wants us to be a part of all of those who know Him – there are no restrictions.

God will place people in your life that will be good for you.

As we meet up and teach each other what we know and are discovering about God and His Kingdom then we will become closer to each other and to God.

It is through this close relationship with a small group that we can then be useful to those around us who don't know Jesus.

The world is a very dark place and we need to be a light in that darkness in order to help them.

We will grow strong as we encourage and teach each other – we will mature as young men and women in God's Kingdom.

We will learn to break down those gates of hell that hold people around us in chains as we mature in this way.

Please don't settle for being just another member of a congregation within a church organisation listening to a 'leader'.

We are called out personally by God Himself – we have a destiny.

We only have one leader and that is God's Spirit. I will talk about Him next.

Baptism in water

When we take that decision to trust in Jesus then immediately God enters our life – we are born again.

This is a phrase that you might be familiar with. It can be a bit of a scary idea for some people – to be born again – what does that really mean?

Jesus was once asked the same question and so I will give you His answer and then explain.

Jesus answered, "Believe me when I say that everyone must be born from water and the Spirit. Anyone who is not born from water and the Spirit cannot enter God's kingdom.

John 3:5 ERV

Jesus said that anyone who isn't born of water and Spirit won't enter God's Kingdom.

When we make the decision to come into God's Kingdom then we are saying that we want to move from one kingdom – the kingdom of darkness, into God's Kingdom - the Kingdom of light.

In order to celebrate and to mark this move we go into the water of baptism – we are baptised into God's Kingdom – our new family.

The waters of baptism are a powerful and a prophetic gesture to mark this occasion.

When we are baptised in water we are declaring that we choose to come under the Lordship of Jesus and we rise up out of the water a new creation in Christ – we have moved into Gods Kingdom.

Baptism in the Spirit

Let us now look at those words of Jesus again:

Jesus answered, "Believe me when I say that everyone must be born from water and the Spirit. Anyone who is not born from water and the Spirit cannot enter God's kingdom.

John 3:5 ERV

We have discussed the first part of this verse – baptism in water; now let's talk about the next thing that Jesus mentioned – baptism in Spirit.

The words that Jesus used were *'born from'* water and Spirit.

When we are baptised we are re-born – baptism is the birthing of a new person.

A miracle of new birth occurs when we are baptised.

We are changed.

What is the connection between baptism in water and baptism in Spirit?

Let's take a look.

One of the last things that Jesus said to His followers before He returned to His Father in heaven was this.

"Remember that I will send you the one my Father promised. Stay in the city until you are given that power from heaven."

Luke 24:49 ERV

Jesus was referring to The Spirit who Father had promised that He would send to be a guide to His followers.

It is Luke who both repeats and gives more detail on what Jesus said at that time in his account in the book of Acts:

One time when Jesus was eating with them, he told them not to leave Jerusalem.

He said, "Wait here until you receive what the Father promised to send. Remember, I told you about it before.

John baptized people with water, but in a few days you will be baptized with the Holy Spirit."

Acts 1:4-5 ERV

Jesus told the disciples to wait in Jerusalem in order to be baptised with the Holy Spirit.

I wonder what they thought was going to happen as they waited?

After all, this was something that had never happened before. It was a new thing.

They couldn't have had much idea at all as to what exactly they were waiting for or what was to happen with them.

I think we are also a little bit like that as we think about baptism.

What will happen? What will it be like? How will it affect me?

There is no need to worry of course because God will never harm us or do anything that will be bad for us.

God will only ever do us good.

In the next chapter of Luke's account we can read what did happen when the promised Spirit came.

I have copied it out for you here:

When the day of Pentecost came, they were all together in one place.

Suddenly a noise came from heaven. It sounded like a strong wind blowing.

This noise filled the whole house where they were sitting. They saw something that looked like flames of fire. The flames were separated and stood over each person there.

They were all filled with the Holy Spirit, and they began to speak different languages. The Holy Spirit was giving them the power to do this.

Acts 2:1-4 ERV

That must have been quite an event mustn't it?

Peter was the first person to realise what was happening and he stood up and explained to those around who were watching.

Peter gave a long explanation telling the people about Jesus and what had happened and finished up by saying

"Change your hearts and lives and be baptized, each one of you, in the name of Jesus Christ.

Then God will forgive your sins, and you will receive the gift of the Holy Spirit.

This promise is for you.

It is also for your children and for the people who are far away. It is for everyone the Lord our God calls to himself."

Acts 2:38-39 ERV

There's that word again – *'everyone'* – this promise is for everyone.

The disciples were baptised in Spirit at that time but the promise is for everyone.

Let's go on to see how baptism in water is linked with baptism in spirit shall we?

Baptism in water and in Spirit.

Let's begin to put these two events together shall we?

There was a time when Paul was on a journey on foot on his way to a place called Ephesus.

Paul came across a group of twelve people who were following the Lord.

As soon as Paul met these followers he noticed that there was something unusual about them. Perhaps it was something in their conversation or perhaps it was their lack of knowledge about Jesus.

I think it was probably because Paul didn't recognise that they had anything of God about them.

Whatever it was Paul sensitively noticed a difference between these people and other followers that he had come across.

Paul enquired whether they had received the Spirit when they were baptised and they told him that they had never heard of baptism of the Spirit.

This puzzled Paul and so he enquired further and asked about their baptism, to which they replied that they had received John (the Baptist) baptism.

When he heard this Paul realised what had happened.

These twelve followers had been baptised by John who had taught them about Jesus - they had been baptised by John as they repented for their way of life but they had moved away after this and hadn't heard about what Jesus had achieved when He gave His life.

They didn't know about being redeemed by Jesus and they didn't know that Jesus had sent His Spirit into the world either.

As soon as Paul had taught them they asked to be baptised into God's Kingdom and immediately afterwards the Spirit fell on them.

I have copied the story from the Bible here for you:

The first thing he asked them was "Did you receive the Holy Spirit when you became believers?"

"No," they replied. "We've not even heard of a Holy Spirit."

Paul asked, "Then what was the meaning of your baptism?"

They responded, "It meant that we would follow John's teaching."

Paul said, "John's baptism was for those who were turning from their sins, and he taught you to believe in and follow the one who was coming after him: Jesus the Anointed One."

When they understood this, they were baptized into the authority of Jesus, the Anointed One.

And when Paul laid his hands on each of the twelve, the Holy Spirit manifested and they immediately spoke in tongues and prophesied.

Acts 19:2-7 TPT

We can see from this event that Paul expected Spirit baptism to naturally follow water baptism with all believers and was surprised when he found these twelve hadn't experienced it.

So much so that he took steps in order to find out the reason and then he put that right.

On another occasion Peter was taken to a house by some men who wanted to know about Jesus. They had heard rumours and wanted to know more.

Peter went and told them about all that Jesus had done.

He told them that Jesus had died and had risen again and that by having faith in Him anyone could be redeemed.

The people listening heard what Peter had to say and immediately believed in the good news.

As Peter was a little hesitant about what to do with these new believers God took control and baptised them in His Spirit.

Peter then realised what he must do in response and baptised them all in water.

The story begins at Acts 10.1. Which you will enjoy reading yourself but I have noted the relevant parts of the story here:

While Peter was speaking, the Holy Spirit cascaded over all those listening to his message.

The Jewish brothers who had accompanied Peter were astounded that the gift of the Holy Spirit was poured out on people who weren't Jews, for they heard them speaking in supernaturally given languages and passionately praising God.

Peter said, "How could anyone object to these people being baptized? For they have received the Holy Spirit just as we have."

So he instructed them to be baptized in the power of the name of Jesus, the Anointed One.

After their baptism, they asked Peter to stay with them for a few more days.

Acts 10:44-48 TPT

We can see then that baptism in water and Spirit is both a natural and also an essential event for a Christian.

Peter was in no doubt that these believers required both.

Baptism is a rebirth .

Through baptism in water and Spirit we become a new creation.

In baptism we are born again into God's Kingdom – into God's family – we become one with God as Spirit takes root within us.

Coming into God's family doesn't come as a result of an emotional response as we are carried along on a tide of euphoria.

When we come into God's Kingdom it should be as a result of a realization of our fallen state and our need of a saviour.

We need to make a conscious decision whether we want to remain as we are – heading towards a lost eternity or do we want to change our way of living and to become one with God as a servant of Jesus?

If you have come to the decision that you want to come into God's Kingdom to be a part of His family then simply tell Him that you have made that choice. He will be delighted; after all, that is why He attracted your attention in the first place, wasn't it?

It will also be a good idea to tell someone else about your decision.

Perhaps you could tell the person who gave you this book?

If you don't know any Christians where you are now then feel free to contact me. My email address is at the end of this book - I will be delighted too!

Q's and A's

Q. Don't Christians believe that God made the world in seven days?

A. Some Christians do believe that but I personally don't and the original phrase in the Bible which is where we get our answers from doesn't say that either.

Where we read in the book of Genesis the word interpreted as *'day'* elsewhere in Genesis the same word has also been interpreted as *'age'* or *'era'*.

Much has been made of the apparent conflict between the Bible and modern science, but, in fact, scientists agree entirely with the order of the development of the universe as related in the account of the creation in Genesis. When we change the word *'day'* for "age" there is no disagreement about the order.

Explanation:

The Bible has been translated by people like you and me who occasionally either make mistakes or believe they have a better understanding of the original text.

Also, very often there is no direct word for word translation for a specific phrase in another language or dialect and therefore the interpreter must draw from their own experience in order to give an approximate meaning.

This has resulted in many incorrectly translated words and/or ideas.

This doesn't mean that the Bible is incorrect or that it has conflicting passages. It means that we need to understand what God is saying in each instance in order to get a proper understanding.

It is only by discovering the very heart of God in line with His word and by cross checking the original phrases that might be found elsewhere in the Bible that we truly begin to understand what the author is trying to convey.

Q. Does it mean that I have to go to church if I become a Christian?

A. The simple answer is no.

When the Bible is translated correctly there is no mention of church at all in it anywhere. The idea of church came some two or three centuries after the time of Jesus and is, quite frankly, often quite the opposite of the plan that God has for us.

It is useful for young Christians to mix with others who are older and wiser in the Kingdom as they will then be able to learn and grow but that is not the same as going to church at all. God has built us into a family and not an organisation.

Q. What is a Christian?

A. The word *'Christian'* means someone who is like Christ – it is a shortened version of the phrase *'Christ-one'*.

When we are baptised and come into God's Kingdom our minds begin to be renewed and restored. Our thoughts change and so do our words and actions.

As we change God's love begins to become a part of our life in greater degrees – we begin to become Christ like.

It is really then that we can be called 'Christian' but modern language and general perspectives have changed since the word was first used and these days we call anyone who is following Jesus a Christian.

Q. Why would I want to become one?

A. We have fallen a long way short of where we should be since the first rebellion of man towards God. So much so that we are often not even aware of our failings or our place in the darkness that engulfs us.

It is not until we take a step into the light that we can look back at where we were and be grateful.

Q. Baptism? Is it necessary?

A. Baptism is necessary if we choose to move from the Kingdom of darkness into God's Kingdom of light.

Baptism is the door through which we travel from one into the other

Q. I was baptised/christened as a child.

A. Baptism into God's Kingdom is a choice that we must make of our own.

When we are baptised as a child our parents make that choice and it signifies nothing.

Q. What happens when we get baptised?

A. I have specifically not mentioned what to expect when we are baptised.

When the Spirit fell on the disciples at Pentecost there appears to have been an element of surprise and then realisation as Spirit became one with them and also as we read the accounts of others being baptised in the bible.

If we have an idea in our head that God is going to do such and such a thing then that becomes our expectation and often we limit God by making assumptions.

What we can say is that whenever we read about baptism in Spirit we also read that He comes with power.

Let that expectation also become ours and allow God to perform what he chooses with us.

We are all different vessels to be filled with new wine as He pleases.

Jesus told the disciples to expect and to wait for the Spirit, so let us also expect and wait for The Spirit.

The Spirit is promised – that is for sure. In our expectation allow God to manifest Himself in our lives as He chooses.

Q. Why is it necessary to be baptised in Spirit?

A. God is Spirit. When we come into God's Kingdom we enter a Spirit fuelled atmosphere – we become a new Spirit filled creation.

It is not possible for us as unchanged people to have a relationship with God.

Spirit enables that change.

Through Spirit baptism we too become one with Spirit – one with God.

Q. What about people who don't get baptised?

A. There are several reasons why some people don't get baptised.

The first person to believe in Jesus was the thief who died on the cross at the same time as Jesus did.

He didn't get baptised because he died shortly afterwards but Jesus said to him that he would be with Jesus in paradise.

Death can be a reason for not being baptised.

Some children die before they are old enough to make a decision for or against God. These won't be baptized either but I have no doubt that there is a place prepared for them.

There are some who decide to follow Jesus but they are never taught about baptism. They live in ignorance. This group miss out on the joy of knowing God in the same way and also the power of living in Spirit – in union with

God but I am sure that their absolute faith will be remembered by God.

I can't bring to mind any reason by way of disability or illness that would make it impossible for a person to be baptised in some fashion but this also may be a reason.

God will judge our hearts.

Others have been taught about baptism but simply don't want to for a variety of reasons. We might wonder about their motivation and whether they are indeed born again if this is their response to God's love and Jesus's sacrifice.

Q. Why did God choose us?

A. This question brings us back to our very first chapter – what is life about?

We were placed on this earth – we evolved under God's guidance because God desires to have a relationship with us.

Quite simply God loves us to bits and we are here in order to have relationship with Him.

God chose each one of us personally – we are handpicked.

When we do not have that relationship then we aren't aware of our purpose on earth and life becomes an endless quest in order to gather more goods, more money or more power.

There is no end to this quest of trying to reach goals - there are always more unattainable goals and life eventually becomes meaningless.

Q. What is our purpose on earth?

A. God desired to have close communion with man – that is still His desire.

We have a commission on earth to bring restoration and to destroy the enemy's influence on the earth.

Jesus gave us the gifts and ability through the power of the Spirit to break down the very gates of hell that hold us and those around us in bondage to sin.

The enemy attempts to persuade us to do things that are bad for us and others. We have the authority to repel those desires and to take back what God wants for us in our lives and also to bring restoration to the fallen world.

We do that by responding to God.

Q. What about other religions?

A. There are many other religions. Most are built upon the lies of the enemy – myths and misunderstandings.

As we begin to have our mind renewed by God's spirit we learn to see through those lies for what they are.

Religions are built around men for the purpose of glorifying man this is manifested in the elaborate buildings that are erected and also by the inanimate objects that are worshipped.

Q. Do I have to pray?

A. Prayer is conversation with God. We talk to God in the same way that we talk to each other. God loves hearing our thoughts and ideas just as any Father would.

Prayer is not reciting phrases over and over. God wants to hear about us and He wants us to learn to hear what He has to say to us as well.

Q. Do I have to sing?

A. No we don't have to sing but we may want to.

Song is normally a response to a thought or emotion.

Many become emotionally lifted by singing in large gatherings such as football and rugby matches or in a choir or even in church.

We might experience Spirit giving us words to sing and also a tune to sing them to. When this happens then it is good to sing with Spirit leading us. This type of song is normally a form of praise or worship but it can also be prophecy or some other gift that God is giving us.

This might occur when we are with others but often at first it might be when we are on our own talking to God.

It may be difficult at first as we are not used to responding to Spirit in this way but as we let Him lead then singing in this way becomes easier.

Very often God will give us a song to sing with words that we don't recognise.

This is called singing in tongues and is one of the gifts of the Spirit.

Song is the response to a joyful heart.

Q. Can anyone come into God's Kingdom?

A. Yes, absolutely anyone can come in. There are no restrictions.

Q. My husband/ wife isn't a Christian what can I do?

A. This can be a very difficult time for us if our spouse is not a believer but it needn't be.

We will experience significant changes in our life which we may not necessarily be able to share easily with the one who is closest to us.

Our spouse will also see that our life style has changed and this may bring confusion and misunderstanding.

It is always better to talk openly about our thoughts and to share what is going on in our lives within a marriage.

Becoming a Christian is the biggest decision that we make – it will be life changing.

It is never God's plan for there to be disagreement or friction between two people who have become one in marriage.

The changes in your life should be for the better for both of you.

You will become a source of new life.

It will be tempting to draw away from your spouse and to spend more time with others in the Kingdom as you make new friends. Do not give in to this temptation. Share your new life with your spouse and introduce them to the new things and people that you are discovering.

In all ways we should serve our spouse and others in love, preferring their wishes above our own desires. This is how we will grow up in love.

As our changes are seen to be positive then we will draw our spouse into a desire to know more about the life of Jesus.

Whatever we do – we will learn to live out of love for others.

There are always further questions and enquiries to be made in the Christian life – everything is new!

There is always something new to discover – something new to share with others.

Please feel free to email me if you have any other questions or would like to talk about this book.

To contact Tim - the author - email:
warwickhouse@mail.com

Tim has also written:

Journey into Life

What did Jesus really preach about when He was on earth?

Within **A Journey into Life** we discover the joy of travelling to a new place.

Tim has set our search for Gods Kingdom in the form of a journey to a new land.

Once inside the new land we begin a journey of discovery – Everything is New.

Did Jesus teach that His Kingdom is within our grasp?

Is this a land – A Kingdom that we can live in now – in our own lifetime?

The answer is yes.

Some Adjustments Required?

We live our lives from day to day carrying out regular routines and rituals often without thinking about what we do and what we say and why .

We take for granted that the things that we have done and said for year upon year and even for centuries past must be right because that is simply the way things are.

Tim has taken some of the many misunderstood concepts in the Christian life that we have for so long taken for granted and brought correction and redirection.

God is doing a new thing in this season and those who want to follow His direction need to hear Him.

EBooks by Tim Sweetman

Journey into Life

Some adjustments required?

A Time To Consider

Other recommended publications of related interest:

By John J Sweetman
EBooks:
Establishing the Kingdom series:
    The Book of Joshua
    The Book of Judges
    The Book of Ruth
    The Book of 1 Samuel
    The Book of 2 Samuel
    The Book of 1 Corinthians
    The Book of 2 Corinthians
    The Book of Galatians
The Emerging Kingdom
Babylon or Jerusalem – your choice
Paperback books:
Babylon or Jerusalem – your choice
The Emerging Kingdom
Establishing the Kingdom series:
    The Book of Joshua
    The Book of Judges
    The Book of Ruth
    The Book of 1 Samuel
    The Book of 2 Samuel
    The Book of 1 Corinthians
    The Book of 2 Corinthians
    The Book of Galatians

by Fiona Sweetman
Paperback and EBook
    Taste the Colour Smell the Number

Printed in Poland
by Amazon Fulfillment
Poland Sp. z o.o., Wrocław